C000253949

AUTUI

Patricia Beer

AUTUMN

CARCANET

First published in 1997 by
Carcanet Press Limited
4th Floor, Conavon Court
12-16 Blackfriars Street
Manchester M3 5BQ

A CIP catalogue record for this book
is available from the British Library
ISBN 1 85754 331 9

The publisher acknowledges financial assistance
from the Arts Council of England

Set in 11pt Garamond Simoncini by Bryan Williamson, Frome
Printed and bound in England by SRP Ltd, Exeter

For Matilda

Contents

Acknowledgements

Some of these poems first appeared in the following publications, to whose editors thanks are due:

London Review of Books
Times Literary Supplement
The Spectator
New Writing: British Council Anthology

AUTUMN

Autumn

Weeds start up out of the wall now that summer has ended.
Holiday-makers already begin to turn yellow.
Shadows look brave but have lost the bone-marrow of August.

Introducing two recently heartbroken friends to each other
How we hope they will mate, how we know that they will not.
The season is over. Young blood has gone into the ground.

In the church a low sun stabs away at the wings of an angel,
That slipped down into darkness last April and stayed there till now,
Making them move, even flap, from their warm hibernation.

Autumn colours walk into our field in the guise of a pheasant,
Bright bronze and with markings like raindrops; respected and safe
Here with us, but the popping of gunfire comes up from the valley,

As it does from a room in the house where somebody is watching
A western. And after the shooting a two-minute silence
For the good and the bad, then the musical ride into sunset.

In the hospital bed that is nearest the door, an old man,
Fenced in by chrysanthemums, blinks out his wife and his sister
And follows the agile young nurse with his eyes, calling 'Mother'.

Ninetieth-Birthday Interview

She still enjoys gardening,
The famous cherry tree she planted
As tall as it will ever get.
Already neighbours and a few relatives
Want her to cut it down.

'Yes, my grandfather was Lord X.
I was a child when the news came.
I told my mother he could not be a Lord
He was not a gentleman.'

Barons wicked but well-bred
Clanked out of books on dark afternoons
Into the firelit nursery.

'Yes, we were rich.
We had nannies and things.
I had about four brothers. Yes.
One died. One was rather tiresome.
One was run over by a horse and cart.
He slipped on some mud crossing the road.'

The dangers of those days.
Loud horses. Silent mud.
But ninety-year-old blood clots
Recalling them.

'Yes. I have one son and one daughter.
Oh yes, my daughter has three children.
No, his wife was rather old,
He has no children.'

Macduff said that.
(She has been a great theatre-goer.)
He knew he would never get his own back
In any sense of the expression,

'What's that?
My son's wife a well-known writer?
Oh yes, she's brainy.
No, she didn't help much with the birthday party,
My grand-daughter Sarah did most of it.
She went to one of those marvellous comprehensive schools,
Her gifts are more social.
My grandson Edward writes,
He's very good indeed.
Oh no, he doesn't *publish*.'

This oral history moves like a bell
Mouth and tongue pealing out notions –
The ring of truth is cracked for ever –
Celebrating only people of the New Year.
Nobody rates a muffled peal.
Husbands seem less dear than departed.

'He died quite a long time ago,
It was a stroke or something,
He had nurses and things.
He did not live to see
My great-granddaughter Carly.'

Treaties, famine, walls coming down,
Traitors, massacres and civil wars
Bore a ninety-year-old pulse.

But the heart opens,
Peeling back like a sardine tin
To show silver grandchildren and great-grandchildren
Beautifully arranged
Lying in state.

Church of the Holy Family

A hot dry afternoon in Spain.
We walk through space that will become a large cool church,
A group of architects and their partners
One of whom mutters that it is ridiculous,
Seeing that religion is on the way out.

There is much talk of what will be where and when,
Less of what is already built:
Rooms full of plans and schemes and models,
Stairs which visitors climb
To look solemnly out of holes
Getting a bird's-eye view
Of a man's dream, rising.
There is nobody working on the site
Who could possibly live to smell the incense.

Tomorrow we go home, back to work,
Back to back in the art galleries of Britain.
And in my case to the cathedral
That I have walked through on and off
For the best part of one of its five centuries
Sheltered from rain and traffic and nonconformists.

My forefathers, soaked to the skin,
Came into market from the sea and the fields
Crossing the transept from south and north
Not for a few seconds like passing under a thick tree –
There was no roof yet –
But because it was the nearest way
To Fish Lane and Colewort Row,

Hallooing to their friends, clanging away above them,
Gossiping about progress
And what their sons and grandsons
Might come to know at last
When air turned into incense
And there was a new king
And perhaps peace and better weather.

At Père Lachaise

October evening. Leaves swoop down like owls
And stun themselves upon the paving-stones.
A skip stands ready for a year of plague.
Patches of fake fur begin to sprout
Upon the clothes of mourning visitors.

Here death smells pleasant, dry like wine not drought.
This cemetery is not a killing field.
It sanctions those who like to make love here
Rather than at home. Its dead are safe.
Their tombs can tumble down above their heads,
Lie there and do no harm. It passes time
Pampering its trees and hierarchy of beasts:
A cat composed of mice and birds and rain
Turns his head, as scornful as a lighthouse.

When is darkness deemed to fall in France,
When do its cemeteries close down for sleep?
Deep in the city, bells are suggesting nightfall
And suddenly beyond a bend in the path
A whistle blows, less loud and much more peevish
Than the Last Trump. A man with a cross face
Comes round the corner, shooing us along.
Husband takes the speckled hand of wife
And they walk back into the world together
Happier than they were, perhaps, in spring.

Sight-seeing in Barcelona

EL PALAU DE LA MUSICA CATALONA

Busts of elegant women
Spring out of the walls
Playing the lute and the harp,
Looking down at their faraway feet
And their two-dimensional flounces.

Ever since we arrived
Someone has been tuning a piano.
We cannot see either of them.
Locate them as east or west,
High or low
Or even be sure they are together.

For the notes uncurl from the china flowers,
Slither round the shining columns,
Skip up the red staircases.
The whole palace is tuning up.

FUNDACIO JOAN MIRO

Gilbert and George
Are the visiting exhibition
Spread out through large spaces
Of sunshine or electric light.

In one small darkish anteroom
A video runs perpetually.
It shows them pouring glasses of wine,
Emptying (not drinking) them
And talking vacuously.

For no reason that I can grasp
The Dead March strikes up
And thuds for ten terrible minutes
To nine empty chairs.

Looking Down at Clifton Suspension Bridge

Up here we are lifesize. The setting sun
Is too. We are all coming in to land.
Down there is I.K. Brunel's bridge, as planned,
Shrunk back into its model, clean and glowing.

We cannot see God's tiny creatures going
On to the middle of the bridge to drop,
And not a single toy Samaritan
Bustles about persuading them to stop.

Ballad of the Underpass

The day I watched them carry her
Along a stony path in Devon,
Black-clothed relations bullied me:
'Now, now, your mother's GONE TO HEAVEN'.

Later I went to read her stone.
The churchyard creaked with lumpy graves.
In all that weight I could not see
The feathery souls that Jesus saves.

I travelled. Time looked after me
The seven seas were nothing to it.
I wanted to make money, love
And war. Time showed me how to do it.

I came home like a story book.
The clock had nothing new to say.
Tractors and cows strolled down the lane
But now time planned a motorway.

It would be almost out of sight
And in itself do little harm
But the approach road would scoop up
The Church and Farmer Gurney's farm.

The Church sent up some peevish prayers.
The farming lobby stood its ground.
A small mob kicked the Ministry
And an alternative was found:

An underpass. The tunnelled road
Is short, the village is so slight.
Today I drove right underneath
The tombstones in the fading light.

'Now I have really GONE ABOVE,'
My mother said, 'though not to Heaven,
Nearer the light, nearer the air.
Set free by half the worms of Devon

My bones hang over you and twitch
Under the rain. Tall as a tree
You used to stand there looking down
And now you must look up at me.'

Poor Ghost

To end a lifetime being called 'Poor Ghost'
By a poor offspring is what hurts the most.

I did not watch enough during my life.
A man desired my kingdom and my wife
And yet I fell asleep, out-of-doors and alone,
Snoring with wine, unshriven. I atone
For blindness now, as well as other wrongs
Down in the flames where ignorance belongs.

Hamlet procrastinates, but I do too.
I am not ghost enough to make him do
What he has sworn. Now he puts on this farce,
This tragedy, simply to make time pass
In which he need not murder Claudius
And I must watch.

                    There stands Polonius
He will call 'Lights' three times. Once would have done.
Windy Polonius, with that fiery son.
He does not watch. He snoops, creatively.
His long nose dimples with delight to see
An arras, for that special mustiness
Goes with his professional success.
I think it is the last thing he will smell.

Now *there* sits one who watches very well.
His fair – as everybody says – young daughter
Has an affinity with running water.
She prattles, snatches flowers as she goes past
And it will be the death of her at last.

Asking good questions: 'What means this, my lord?'
She may not follow but she is not bored.
She thinks the prologue may explain the plot.
Hamlet likes dirty puns but she does not
And tends, when he is making them, to say,
Changing the subject, 'I will mark the play'.
And so she does and not the play alone
But everything that may be going on.
'The King rises.' She states the obvious.
But someone has to. Nobody else does.
The time will come when she will hold the floor.
Courtiers will watch *her* in *her* play, no more
The curly little ewe that no one tups.
The script will then announce 'Enter the corpse'.

Here comes the Queen, not mine in any sense.
A lifelong member of the audience,
Not watched herself she thinks subjectively.
Her comments are unheard by all but me:
About the 'Queen's' performance: 'Purest ham.
That woman is less clever than I am.'
True. She kept quiet at her second wedding,
Ignoring jokes about leftovers, bedding
With Claudius to be the Queen again.
I never let her go out in the rain.
I am the husband who is dead but walks
(She overhears and everybody talks)
Among the wet towers high above the sea.
'He never comes indoors to comfort me.'
She has stepped out of love as I have done
And takes her place where she can watch her son.

That man there, my son's friend Horatio,
Watches what other people want him to.
He does not sit with Hamlet at the play
Yet afterwards he knows just what to say:
'Ay, my lord, I did note him very well',
Agreeing with him all the way to hell.
The King will need him when Ophelia
Cries out good-night at noon and goes her way.
'Give her good watch, I pray you,' he will call.
Hamlet will need him too, and so will all
The scheming dead ones among whom he dies.
Horatio is the man who trusts his eyes
And knows he saw me yet is not the one
To convince Hamlet, my agnostic son,
Who thinks that he may not have seen the ghost
Though he has far more evidence than most.
Horatio, the witness, cannot die.
He must agree to live. 'Ay, my lord, ay.'

Just look at Claudius, watching that pair
As they strut love before the poisoner
Comes on. He smiles and nods as a king ought
But then his smile slides back into his throat,
His nod begins to shake. He knows I walk
And probably assumes that I can talk
And might tell some dim-witted sentry how
He killed me in my garden. But I know
He is prepared to scoff: 'A likely tale
With gardeners about.' That news is stale.
His spies reported it some weeks ago.
Now he has guessed I told his nephew so.
His spies have also made sure that he knows
How I start guiltily when the cock crows
And how as the sea re-appears I smell

The coming day and hurry back to hell.
I must be much more evil than men say,
He thinks, deciding he must watch and pray.

I who perceive the ending have no strength
To alter it. I plead and fret. At length
Silence will come back once the play is done.
I shall return to gather up my son
When he and Claudius and all are dead.
When he was young I carried him to bed.
In life I could not lift a full-grown man
But ghosts are strong as graves and now I can.

Folk Remedies

'Three times round the gasworks'
In my childhood
This was the prescription
For a persistent cough.

To go three times round ours
My grandmother regularly
From Christmas to Spring
Came across the river
In the stout-hearted little ferry.

Another prescription was
To go up in an aeroplane.

Superstitions both, and useless.
But at least the first remedy
Was accessible to anyone
Who lived within reach of gasworks.

As to the second, only one person
In a million, if that,
Could afford to fly.

Green Christmas

Christmas will be green,
Snow locked up this year,
No white background for crows.
We shall celebrate here

Concentrating on green.
I ask what kind of tree,
Get as many views as guests:
Fifteen. Here are three.

'A small token branch:
Just one fallen bird,
The flock still flying.
Unless you are God

And count everything
There is no diminution.'
'A fine whole tree
In our fathers' fashion.

Dug up with its roots
It may live again later
Or with them burnt right off
It will hold the sap better.'

'An artificial tree
By factory out of shop.
They last forever.
No needles, no leaves drop.'

They shall all have what they choose,
Quot homines tot sententiae
Each notion satisfied
Revelling in greenery.

Mine

A two-car family
Lived half-way up a winding hill
Which devoured ashes in ice-time.

Husband and wife
Had a boxful each
Which they guarded like Cerberus;
Big caskets, not like those
Which emerge from the crematorium,
Tiny containers full of large people.

One black December
A friend came to stay
And dug his way
Without a by-your-leave
Into the silver-grey treasure
Hoarded by the wife, Theresa.

Her loving husband
Knowing her possessiveness
And how the infiltration hurt her
Took a pencil hard as a stiletto
And gouged into the cardboard
The words 'Theresa's ashes'.

Street Scene

'What are you all waiting here for?' she said
Coming round the corner with her shopping.

The gates to the Underground were shut
And steel blinds crept carefully down
The windows of jewellers' shops,
Guillotines in slow motion.

She was expecting a princess with a child or two
But death was waiting in a piece of left luggage.

Ruritanian uniforms ran
Between one vehicle and another.
The excitement set off an alarm in the bank.
'Move along there'
Shouted the more familiar police.

But we waited,
For death or a princess to come out into the open.

Lizzie

Strip by strip, Christina Rosetti is pasting
Pieces of paper over the most arousing lines
Of the poet Swinburne. Soon she will start
To investigate the respectful, formal
Applications of the many composers
Who wish to set her poems to music,
To make sure they are *normal*.

Engraving is different and Gabriel is her brother.
There they lie, just as she said,
The two girls who went down to the goblins' market,
Golden head to golden head,
But also goitrous throat to goitrous throat
And a large hand fondling a large shoulder.
A bright porthole reveals the goblins,
Bounding downhill, fat, comical, childish.
Wicked men should look older.

How old did the snake look in the Garden of Eden
When he pressed sensuous fruit on the first girl?
Down in the glen when light was shrinking
And the dew swelling, there was no question about it:
Laura was tempted and ate, juicily.
Critics have said that the fluids were religious heresies.
Somehow I doubt it.

The good sister, who fought cool as snow against goblin passion,
Christina Rosetti called Lizzie. It was the name
Of Gabriel's long-time mistress
Who had been very faithful to him after her fashion.

Art History

I am the man in the pink hat
Who catches everybody's eye
And is not really there.

In the preparatory version
My hat was dowdy,
I was older.
Now I am 'Who is that good-looking man?'
My brim is wide and bumptious,

I am immune, although hemmed in
By people working miracles,
Waving their arms about
In paeans of caring.

I am better-dressed
Than goody-two-sleeves, Francis Xavier.
My robe is off-white silk
And pours down me like warm rain.
His is black and catches on his bones.

I hate do-gooders,
I believe the Good Samaritan
Sprang from behind a sharp rock
And mugged the man who famously went down
From Jerusalem to Jericho.
At the right moment he returned
With oil and wine and succour
And lives forever.

Francis Xavier is bound to get to heaven
And he will no doubt pray for me
If I and my pink dynasty of hats
Are spared like late roses.
I have no heart for others
He has none for himself.

Look, the dead rise up as white as candles,
With flame-coloured hair.
There is no room nor breath for them,
The air is stuffed with angels.
I am not giving up my place,
I have none,
Though I am central to this resurrection.

From Wilfred Owen 1918

Dear Mother, now I am no more
A fighting man, I warm the plates
And make some bugler black the grates.
We are all soldiers far from war.

The foremost object in our minds
Is blacking out the Scarborough lights.
I turn back from the sea at nights
To check the drawing-down of blinds.

My dearest Mother, I can scare
The Mess by going to their dance.
They heard that I was killed in France.
Ashes and crumbs lie everywhere.

Doctors pronounce. I bow to them.
They tell me I am fit to serve.
War dreams return to every nerve.
We go on board at 3 p.m.

Now I have brought my lowing kine
Once more along this ancient track,
I am not sorry to be back.
Tomorrow we go up the line.

In action now. My uniform
Is bright with someone else's blood.
He fell across me in the mud
And he grew cold. My hand is warm

Enough to write DECEASED on those
I led. Dearest of Mothers, I
Begin to think I may not die.
The war is drawing to a close,

My own sweet Mother. Monday's dead
May be the last. That crimson stain
Has turned to sepia.
                          I remain
Ever your loving son, Wilfred.

Small Talk at Wreyland

(in memory of Cecil Torr)

It is hard to believe that he lived till the rise of the Nazis
And the General Strike and nine or ten Armistice Days
And that I was a child putting flowers on my grandmother's grave
Three churchyards away on the day that he died.

His forebears had gossiped their hold on the centuries.
One of them spotted Napoleon on the Bellerophon,
Moored in Torbay, with its prisoner stumping morosely
About on the deck; worldwide Boney, not looking his best.

Torr himself saw Garibaldi processing through London
As well as a Sultan, a King and two French elder statesmen,
But not half as plain as the Devil who hid in the bracken
Beside Yarner Wood, or a group of spiritual men
(As they used to call ghosts on the moors), or a stranger
Seen taking a little-known path to the top of a tor.

Never whimsical, even when speaking of saints like Sebastian
And Pancras who after their swim in the river of Paradise
Sat on a sunny bank drying their haloes.
He was sceptical; when the good men of Assisi
Described how St Francis knelt groaning in prayer all night long
He said with some reverence that Francis was probably snoring.
He was lazy himself except on his travels abroad.
He was cynical likewise: he felt that the clever embezzlers
And wayward but brilliant financiers imprisoned on Dartmoor
Might be asked to take over the work of his own District Council,
An honest but deeply incompetent body of men
Who had just spent five pounds on a signpost which got it all wrong,
Sending people to Wreyland instead of the station.

He watched Brunel's railway advancing (I watched it retreating)
Drumming its way up the valley from Newton to Moreton.
To begin with, his feelings were mixed, for it paid well and lured
The farm labourers out of their fields. But he came to enjoy it:
The evening train hooted on leaving the station
On its way to the plain, and the owls hooted back.
Engines had names and he met them all over the world.
He once saw Lars Porsena letting off steam outside Clusium.

The First World War seemed to mean little to him, being neither
Crimean nor Boer nor connected with Boney.
He scattered allusions: a boy who played tricks
On the spinsters of Lustleigh was killed in a battle, the name
Of which no one remembered; a wounded old friend of the author
Had married his nurse; on Armistice morning at Bovey
A flag had got stuck at half-mast after four years of killing.
He remarked that the prisoners-of-war in the neighbouring fields
Looked like the farmers' sons working beside them.
Well, they would, wouldn't they? Saxon blood, probably.
But he got angry about the Memorial, genteel and safe
Installed in the church, for he felt that the dead deserved granite
Somewhere up there on the tor which hung on to the light
Long after the Cleave was as dark and as wet as a trench.

Our paths almost crossed in the way that paths do on the moors.
He was interested in the name Beer and discussed it at length.
He believed it identified people who lived near a wood.
(In the days of surnaming it would have been difficult not to.)
My grandmother's people were natives of Chagford.
If she had not decided to go to Torquay
And enter good service, she might have been Cecil Torr's housemaid,
Streamering up to his room with a ewer of hot water.

He ended his small talk with thoughts of the little volcano
That long ago sneezed in what now is his parish, with dreams
Of a time when the soft parts of Dartmoor would sink in the sea
And the granite which held his house up in the air all those years
Would have turned into Wreyland, a reef on an up-to-date chart
Much respected by shipping and always made brilliant by waves.

I wish he could talk to me now that the day is declining
And the spiritual men are preparing to walk on the moors,
Talk about chimneys and highwaymen, talk about anything.
They say I have symptoms which can be controlled but not cured.
I am the same age as he was when chatting his way
Into darkness, his notions cavorting around him like fireflies.

House-warming Present

I am a lion. I am yours.
I could be living out of doors
At one-two-five St Stephen's Way,
Couchant for ever and a day,
If you would like me to. A man
Will bring me in a sort of van.

I am a lion. Every part
Of me is stone, except my heart.
I will be loyal, brave and true
And guard you always, all of you.
Think of me as your friend outside
And you indoors shall be my pride.

Millennium

A thousand times travelling over these fields,
Shorn as if shamed, the shortest day
Has yellowed and gone, yomping to new year.
From a Wessex window we have watched it.
We mull over the millennium. Not many days now.

This time ten centuries ago
(Romans retired, Normans not ready)
Saxons had come here to settle, not swallow or govern.
Vain in vigour they vowed this hill would suit them.
Wood served these warlords wonderfully for dwelling.
They lived off the land, lopping the trees
That soared again in the same spot, as mead-halls
Where warriors wilted, weapons erect beside them.
They snored, serging and slumping with the verse,
Pleased the poet. They performed his rhythm.
Bats burst in out of a burning night sky
Like stars scorched and scattered over Middle-earth.

At sunrise they would set out to seek more land,
Claiming Cornwall, calling its fields after themselves.
Half-foemen, half farmers, they frisked like centaurs
On the Roman road that rang through Exeter,
Till moors muffled them and mists sent wandering.

Paganism was patchy but powerful nonetheless
Giving new greatness to the goddess Easter.
Kings of Wessex were Christians, counting their years
From the birth. Backsliders, brought home by carols
Each winter, kept Woden but worshiped one God.

Fifty fathers-and-sons fill this place,
Heroes hidden in earth or hoarded offshore
Tombed with their treasures till tides parted them
They left us language and lymph, verse
Made of sibling sounds and strong heartbeats.
We have always talked of lasting till Two Thousand.
From January on we could join them, justly,
For now comes Nunc Dimittis, if needed.
It is dispiriting to dodge death for ever.

SEQUENCE

Private Wing in July

Night with its epileptic dreams
Is over, and for once there seems

To be some flavour in the day.
Outside my room – my territory

Where the seasons do not enter –
The dawn chorus of the nurses (banter

About the night and how it went)
Seems to give off a kind of scent.

Consultants come round early here.
Out-of-doors must be getting near.

And here they are, dressed for their parts
In laundered cotton poplin shirts.

Doors open for them. They disperse,
Each to a room, trailing a nurse.

They smell of grass where there is none
And distant rivers in the sun,

Of picnics and al fresco sin.
Summer is icumen in.

Visitor

My window at the hospital
Overlooks the car park, full

As a market at this time of day
With patients who have got away:

Spouses being bundled home.
Later the visitors will come,

To see the Sabine women left
Behind unwanted, faces daft

As daisies peering out at life.
I view the matter as a wife

For now a car drives in and takes
Its place, as every day for weeks,

Silver powdered down to pearl
By summer lanes and plants that hurl

Their seeds at every passer-by.
A man is getting out whom I

Stood beside thirty years ago
And heard agreeing to be true

In sickness and in health. He is
The man who said 'I will'. And has.

Tongue-tied

I was born tongue-tied. Ages later
Here comes once more the suffocator

That I cannot recall but must
Have been what paralysed me most

Of all the things I could not do.
My speech is back in prison now.

Whatever silenced me when young
Has put a thimble on my tongue.

Recovery Room

The noise in the recovery room
Was half footfall and half hum

Like a well-mannered gallery
Of pictures that I could not see.

And then a name disrupted it:
The hated name of childhood: Pat,

A name I had not answered to
For fifty years and would not now.

Another voice began to talk:
Pat. And still I did not speak.

My husband waited in my room
And in the end they sent for him,

After an hour or two of this.
I heard Patricia. And said 'Yes?'

Post-operative Confusion

Back home. Sixty years dead my mother
Is chattering downstairs. My father

Is in the kitchen making tea
As if this domesticity

Would prove that he had never been
A child-abuser or profane,

Both of them very idle fears.
He has been dead thirty-five years.

They came in on the rising tide
To meet their daughter who had died.

That is what they must have done
And very soon they will have gone

Away, silently and forgiving.
This is my house. Where I am living.

Convalescence

I am on my own My husband
Is away (and I am housebound)

Seeing his mother, ninety-five.
He found her less dead than alive,

Gardening, before the sun
Got warmer than the air and when

The grass still smelled of night and fear.
She was preparing for New Year,

Planting early bulbs that looked
Scaly, mauve and undercooked.

She has not buried them in vain.
And some sick people rise again.

Too Deep for Tears

After two illnesses last year
I find I cannot shed a tear

At *Little Women* in the spring.
The book provided everything

That made grown men a century
Ago wring out their beards. Today

The film holds nothing back. We have
Gentle dying words, a grave,

A pet canary in its shroud,
A battered much-loved doll, a crowd

Of people running into other
People's arms, a song, a father

In some place where the fighting is,
Christmas snow and families.

I have just left hospital.
This outing signals my recall

To normal life and I am glad
(Having expected to be dead),

So are my family, for me,
Yet they weep unrestrainedly

And I cannot. I have known illness
Like a truth in all its fullness.

Things just kept happening and I
Allowed them to. Drips standing by,

Needles approaching, every spasm,
I welcomed them as realism.

Every procedure was a fact.
No need to fantasise or act.

A year of actuality
Has almost dehydrated me.